DATE DUE

MR 09 '04			

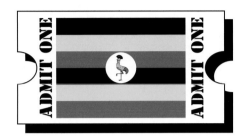

Villagers
Riding
Bicycles In
Nakaseke

FACES
AND
PLACES

UGANDA

BY ELMA SCHEMENAUER

THE CHILD'S WORLD®

COVER PHOTO

A young girl in Kawempe.
©Liba Taylor/CORBIS

Published in the United States of America by The Child's World®
PO Box 326
Chanhassen, MN 55317-0326
800-599-READ
www.childsworld.com

Project Manager James R. Rothaus/James R. Rothaus & Associates
Designer Robert E. Bonaker/R. E. Bonaker & Associates
Contributors Mary Berendes, Dawn M. Dionne, Katherine Stevenson, Ph.D., Red Line Editorial

Library of Congress Cataloging-in-Publication Data
Schemenauer, Elma.
Uganda / by Elma Schemenauer.
p. cm.
Includes index.
ISBN 1-56766-914-X (library bound : alk. paper)
1. Uganda—Juvenile Literature.
[1. Uganda]
I. Title.
DT433.222 .S34 2003
967.61—dc21

00-013187

Table of Contents

If you were a giant bird soaring high above Earth, you would see huge land areas with water around them. These land areas are called **continents**. Uganda is in the eastern part of the continent of Africa. The **equator**, an imaginary line around the middle of Earth, runs through Uganda.

Western Hemisphere

Eastern Hemisphere

Uganda (white) is in the east and U.S.A. (green) is in the west

Uganda has five neighboring countries—Sudan to the north, Kenya to the east, Tanzania and

Rwanda to the south, and the Democratic Republic of the Congo to the west. Uganda has no seacoast, but it includes almost half of Lake Victoria, Africa's largest lake. Lake Victoria is a source of the world's longest river, the Nile.

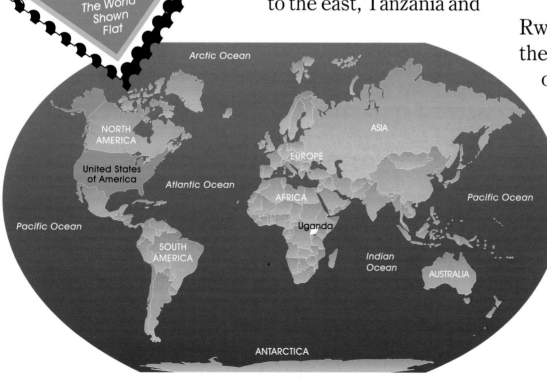

The World Shown Flat

Arctic Ocean

NORTH AMERICA

United States of America

Atlantic Ocean

Pacific Ocean

ASIA

EUROPE

AFRICA

Uganda

Pacific Ocean

SOUTH AMERICA

Indian Ocean

AUSTRALIA

ANTARCTICA

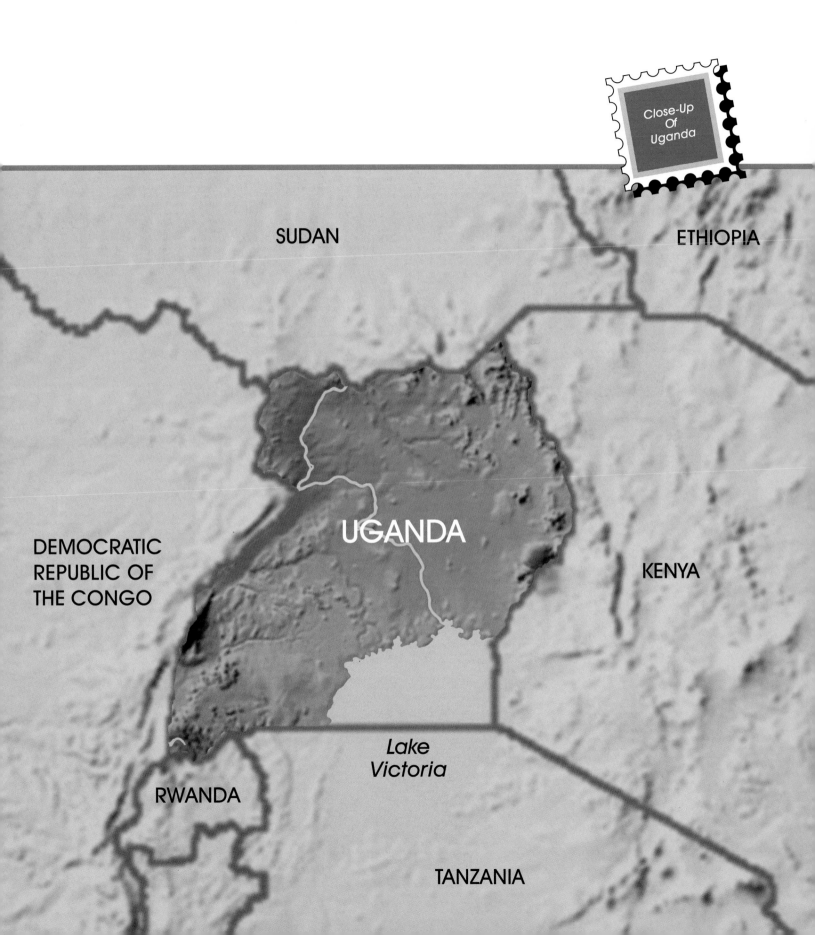

SUDAN

ETHIOPIA

DEMOCRATIC
REPUBLIC OF
THE CONGO

UGANDA

KENYA

RWANDA

*Lake
Victoria*

TANZANIA

Murchison Falls

Murchison Falls National Park

LAKE KWANIA
LAKE BISINA
LAKE ALBERT
LAKE KYOGA
• Nakaseke
Rwenzori Mountains
LAKE EDWARD
LAKE VICTORIA

©Ric Ergenbright/CORBIS

Hantebeasts On a Savanna

© The Purcell Team/CORBIS

Much of Uganda is made up of high plains. These plains include rolling hills and flat grasslands called **savannas**. The country sits in a cradle of mountains, with mountain ranges making up long stretches of its borders. The Rwenzori Mountains along the western border are often called the "Mountains of the Moon" because of their height. They are so high that snow and ice stay on some peaks all year round.

A Fertile Valley In Uganda

British government leader Winston Churchill once called Uganda the "Pearl of Africa" because of its great beauty. Today some people call Uganda the "Land of Lakes." Do you know why? Besides Lake Victoria, Uganda's lakes include Lakes Albert, Edward, Kyoga, Kwania, and Bisina. The lakes help keep Uganda's weather cool.

©Papilio/CORBIS

9

Most of Uganda gets lots of rain, so it has lush green grasses and forests of evergreens and other trees. Water plants such as papyrus often grow in the swampy areas around the lakes. Only the northeastern part of Uganda is dry. There, thorn bushes and cactuses are the main plants.

Among Uganda's many animals are crocodiles, hippopotamuses, water buffalo, warthogs, antelopes, giraffes, and elephants. Red-tailed monkeys and chimpanzees are among its **primates**. Uganda's best known primates are mountain gorillas. Only a few hundred mountain gorillas are left in the world. Ugandans want to protect their mountain gorillas and make sure they do not die out.

©Joe McDonald/CORBIS

A Female Mountain Gorilla

©Staffan Widstrand/CORBIS

A Hippopotamus In Queen Elizabeth National Park

©Staffan Widstrand/CORBIS

Kibale Forest
National Park
Queen Elizabeth
National Park
LAKE
VICTORIA

The Kabaka
Of Uganda
In 1928

NILE RIVER

Kampala ★

LAKE
VICTORIA

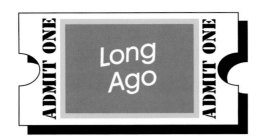

Long Ago

Long ago several different groups of African people hunted, herded animals, and farmed in what is now Uganda. Some peoples, including the Baganda and Basoga, set up kingdoms to rule certain areas. Sometimes they fought over those areas.

Arab traders, European explorers, and Christian **missionaries** arrived in the 1800s. One European country, Great Britain, set up **protectorates** in the area.

Great Britain promised to protect the groups' chiefs from their enemies in return for trade and cooperation. In time, Great Britain began ruling the whole area through the Bagandan chiefs and their king, or *kabaka*.

Guards Outside The Ugandan Palace Gateway

Ugandan President Yoweri Museveni

On October 9, 1962, Uganda became a country of its own, and Ugandans began running their own government. The first president was the Bagandan king, Kabaka Edward Mutesa II. However, prime minister Milton Oboto drove him out and made himself president. In 1971 an army leader, Idi Amin, chased Oboto out and used the army to rule by force. Amin wasted the country's wealth and killed people who did not agree with him.

In 1979 Amin was driven out and Oboto came back. Oboto, however, ran Uganda as badly as Amin had. In 1985 the army overthrew Oboto, and in 1986 President Yoweri Museveni took over. At last Uganda had a better leader. Museveni has been trying to keep order, rebuild the country, and help the people.

©David & Peter Turnley/CORBIS

President Idi Amin, Ruler Of Uganda During The 1970s

©Bettmann/CORBIS

NILE RIVER

Kampala ★

LAKE VICTORIA

Mutebi, Kabaka Of The Ganda People

Smiling
Children In
Kampala

NILE RIVER

Kampala ★

LAKE
VICTORIA

A Ugandan Man Wearing A Head Cloth In Kampala

Uganda's population is made up of three main African groups. The largest, the Bantu people, live in southern Uganda. The Bantu include the Baganda, Basoga, and Banyankole peoples. Of these, the Baganda make up the largest part of Uganda's population. In fact, the name Uganda means "land of the Baganda." Besides the Bantu, the other main African groups are the Nilotics, whose name comes from the Nile River, and the Sudanics. Both the Nilotics and Sudanics live mainly in the north.

The country also has small numbers of other Africans, including Pygmies. Uganda's non-Africans include Europeans and Arabs. Uganda used to include a number of Asian businesspeople, but President Idi Amin drove them out in 1972. He thought Uganda's businesses should be run by Africans. In recent years some Asians have returned.

©David & Peter Turnley/CORBIS

A Woman Carrying A Basket On Her Head

©David & Peter Turnley/CORBIS

ADMIT ONE

City Life
And
Country
Life

ADMIT ONE

In the country, many Ugandans live in houses with iron or thatched roofs, and mud, wood, or cement walls. Some city people also live in houses like these. In large cities, many people live in apartments or in small houses with wide porches. The larger cities in Uganda are much like other cities around the world, with tall buildings, markets, and busy streets.

A Large City In Uganda

©David & Peter Turnley/CORBIS

Ugandans Riding In A Truck

©David Turnley/CORBIS

Among both country and city people, a number of Ugandans suffer from the disease called AIDS. Thousands of children have no homes because both of their parents have died from the disease. Scientists have not yet found a cure for AIDS. Ugandan government leaders and others are teaching people how to protect themselves and stop the spread of this deadly disease.

Soroti

LAKE VICTORIA

©Caroline Penn/CORBIS

Students Writing In Class Near Luwero

Luwero
Mpigi
LAKE VICTORIA

©David Turnley/CORBIS

A Schoolboy Carrying Books In Mpigi

©Caroline Penn/CORBIS

Ugandan children attend primary school for 7 years. They can then attend 4 years of high school and 2 years of higher education. After that, they can go to a university. Schools are important to Ugandans, but not all children have a chance to attend. Even if they do, their schools are often short of books and teachers. Many students go to school for only a few years.

Schools are taught mainly in Uganda's official language, English. Another important language is Swahili, used in businesses all over eastern Africa. A third language is Luganda, the language of the Baganda people. People in Uganda also speak a number of other languages, including Arabic.

A Teacher And Students Near Luwero

©David & Peter Turnley/CORBIS

Work

About 80 percent of Ugandans are farmers and planters. Crops grown mainly for food include bananas, corn, millet, beans, sweet potatoes, and cassava (used to make bread and **tapioca**). Other crops, especially coffee, cotton, tea, and sugarcane, are grown mainly to sell. Animals raised include cattle and goats.

Bricklayers Hard At Work

©David & Peter Turnley/CORBIS

A Man Working In A Factory

©David & Peter Turnley/CORBIS

Some Ugandans mine copper and other minerals. Others fish in the lakes and rivers. Some people work in factories making cloth, food products, plywood, cement, and other goods. Some Ugandans have jobs taking care of visitors, or **tourists,** from other countries who come to see Uganda's mountain gorillas and other wild animals. In the cities a number of Ugandans work in stores, banks, and offices.

LAKE
VICTORIA

Harvesting Tea
Leaves

A Boy
Carrying
Bananas In
Mbarara

• Gulu

Mbarara •

LAKE
VICTORIA

©Caroline Penn/CORBIS

Food

Ugandans eat mostly foods produced in their own country. They grow and eat many different kinds of bananas. These include bananas for eating raw, bananas for roasting or frying, and green bananas.

Green bananas, called *matoke,* are often tied inside a bundle of banana leaves and then steamed and mashed. Matoke might be eaten with beans or with a beef, goat, or mutton stew that also contains vegetables. Another dish eaten with beans or stew is cornmeal cooked until thick and then cut into flat slices.

Other foods often eaten in Uganda include millet bread, fresh fruit, and freshwater fish, including huge perch from the Nile River. Drinks include milk, soft drinks, coffee, tea, and beer.

A Boy Cooking In Gulu

©Liba Taylor/CORBIS

Ugandans enjoy music, dancing, art, plays, and storytelling. Games and sports are also popular. One favorite game is *Omweso,* played by two people using a board with rows of holes. They place shiny black seeds in the holes, then follow rules to try to capture each other's seeds. Among other popular pastimes are chess, basketball, golf, soccer, rugby, car racing, and motorcycle racing.

Holidays include New Year's Day on January 1, International Women's Day on March 8, Independence Day on October 9, and Christmas on December 25. On Eid al Adha, **Muslims**, who make up about 16 percent of Uganda's population, remember the **prophet** Abraham's strong faith in God.

June 3 is Martyrs' Day. On that day **Christians**, who make up about 65 percent of the population, remember 20 brave Ugandans who gave their lives for their faith in 1886.

Uganda has gone through gloomy times, but its people are strong and hopeful. They are working to make their beautiful land, the Pearl of Africa, shine once again.

A Vatussi Dance

©Fulvio Roiter/CORBIS

©Fulvio Roiterl/CORBIS

Gulu
Kampala
Entebbe
Jinja
Mbale
LAKE VICTORIA

Bwindi Impenetrable Forest National Park

Villagers Preparing For A Celebration

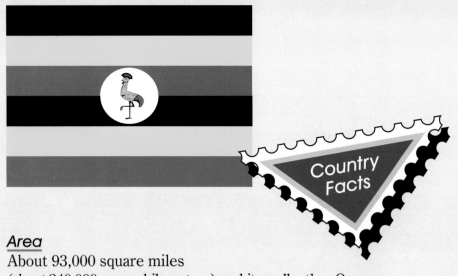

Area
About 93,000 square miles
(about 240,000 square kilometers)—a bit smaller than Oregon.

Population
About 20 million people.

Capital City
Kampala.

Other Important Cities
Jinja, Entebbe, Mbale, and Gulu.

Money
The Uganda shilling, which is divided into 100 cents.

Official Name
The Republic of Uganda.

National Flag
The flag has six sideways stripes. The black stripes stand for Africa. The yellow stripes stand for sunshine, and the red ones for brotherhood. In the center of the flag stands a crested crane.

National Bird
The crested crane.

National Song
"Oh! Uganda, May God Uphold Thee."

National Holiday
Independence Day on October 9.

Head of Government
The president of Uganda.

A Shoebill Stork

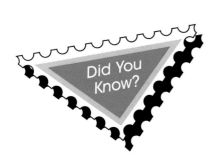

Uganda
Trivia

ADMIT ONE   ADMIT ONE

Visitors can view mountain gorillas in Uganda's Bwindi Impenetrable Forest. But people must be careful not disturb the shy primates.

Ugandans make and play many kinds of drums. In the past they sent messages by pounding out rhythms on "talking" drums. One drum rhythm would tell children to run home because danger was near. Another would ask neighbors to come and help harvest crops.

The water hyacinth is a problem in Uganda. This pretty, fast-growing plant is clogging the shores of Lake Victoria and the Nile River. It covers the surface of the water, making it hard for ships to sail into ports. It also cuts off oxygen needed by fish.

The name of Uganda's capital city, Kampala, means "hill of impalas or antelopes."

How
Do You
Say?

	SWAHILI	*HOW TO SAY IT*
Hello	jambo	JAHM–boh
Good-bye	kwa heri	kwa–HAIR–ee
Please	tafadhali	tah–fah–DAH–lee
Thank You	asante	ah–SAHN–tay
One	moja	MOH–ja
Two	mbili	mm–BEE–lee
Three	tatu	TAH–too
Uganda	Uganda	yoo–GAHN–dah

Glossary

Christians (KRISS-chenz)
Christians believe that Jesus Christ was God's son. Christians make up about 65 percent of Uganda's population.

continents (KON-tih-nents)
Continents are huge areas of land surrounded mostly by water. Uganda is in the eastern part of the continent of Africa.

equator (ee-KWAY-ter)
The equator is an imaginary line that divides Earth in half. Countries that lie on or near the equator have warm weather all year long. Uganda lies on the equator.

missionaries (MIH-shun-ayr-eez)
Missionaries are people who teach and do good works (on behalf of a religious group), often in faraway countries. Missionaries came to Uganda in the 1800s.

Muslims (MOOHS-lemz)
Muslims follow the religion of Islam. About 16 percent of Ugandans are Muslims.

primates (PRY-mates)
Primates are a group of intelligent mammals that include monkeys, apes, and people. Uganda's best-known primates are mountain gorillas.

prophet (PRAHF-et)
A prophet is a person who speaks on God's behalf. Some people believe that a man named Abraham was a prophet long ago.

protectorates (proh-TEK-tor-ets)
Protectorates are weak states or territories that are partly controlled and protected by a stronger state or country. The country of Great Britain set up protectorates in Uganda in the 1800s.

savannas (suh-VAN-nuz)
Savannas are hot, dry grasslands with a few trees and shrubs. Parts of Uganda are covered with savannas.

tapoica (tap-ee-OH-kuh)
Tapioca is the juice or pulp of the cassava plant. It is used in many Ugandan dishes.

tourists (TOOR-ists)
Tourists are visitors and vacationers to another country. Some Ugandans have jobs taking care of tourists.

Index

Web Sites

Learn more about Uganda!

Visit our homepage for lots of links about Uganda:
http://www.childsworld.com/links.html

Note to Parents, Teachers, and Librarians:
We routinely verify our Web links to make sure they're safe,
active sites—so encourage your readers to check them out!